Happy Elephants

Rob Waring, *Series Editor*

HEINLE
CENGAGE Learning

Australia • Brazil • Japan • Korea • Mexico • Singapore • Spain • United Kingdom • United States

Words to Know

This story is set in the United States (U.S.). It happens in the state of Maryland, in a city called Baltimore.

A **Elephants in the Wild.** Read the facts about elephants. Then, write each underlined word or phrase next to the correct definition.

> When elephants are <u>in the wild</u>, they are free.
> Elephants live in families, like <u>humans</u> do.
> Several elephant families often come together to make a <u>herd</u>.
> When it is hot, elephants like to get into water and <u>mud</u>.
> Elephants use their <u>trunk</u> to pick up things.

1. a soft combination of water and earth: _____

2. people: _____

3. the long powerful nose of an elephant: _____

4. in natural conditions: _____

5. a large group of animals of the same type that live and eat together: _____

A Herd of Elephants

B Elephants at Work.

Elephants at Work. Look at the pictures and read the paragraph. Then, complete the paragraph with the words in the box.

gentle	captivity	trainer	circus	zoo

If elephants aren't in the wild, they are usually in (1) _____ and are kept by people. These elephants often live in a zoo or work in a circus. A (2) _____ is a place where many animals live and people can go to see them. Many people love elephants because they're usually very friendly and (3) _____. Other elephants work in a (4) _____. This is a kind of show in which people and animals perform. An animal (5) _____ works with these elephants. This person teaches the elephants what to do in the show.

An Elephant in the Zoo

An Animal Trainer with a Circus Elephant

E lephants are very large animals, but they are also very gentle. They are important to humans too. Elephants and people have worked together for over 2,000 years. However, when they work with people, the elephants are usually not in the wild. They are usually in captivity and working in zoos or circuses.

Over these 2,000 years, people have learned a lot about the way elephants act. However, there is one question that people are still concerned about: How can people keep elephants happy when they are in captivity?

 CD 1, Track 03

4

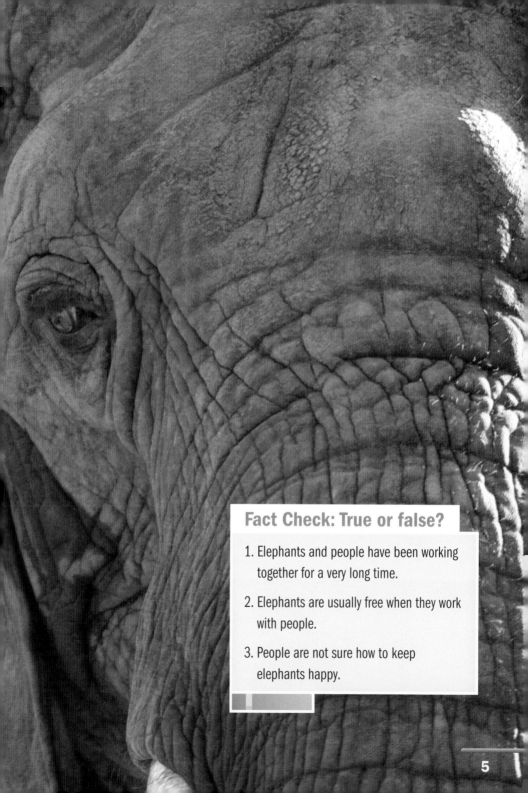

Fact Check: True or false?

1. Elephants and people have been working together for a very long time.

2. Elephants are usually free when they work with people.

3. People are not sure how to keep elephants happy.

Mike **Hackenberger**[1] is a skilled animal trainer at the Baltimore Zoo. He works hard to make sure his elephants are healthy and seem happy. His elephants even seem to say 'hello' when Hackenbergers says, "OK, everyone, trunk foot salute!"

"We make sure teeth are where they're supposed to be, [they] don't have **ingrown feet**[2]..." he explains. "This is all that good **husbandry**[3] stuff," he adds. Hackenberger is responsible for teaching other zoo workers how to recognize a happy elephant. Part of his method for doing this is to talk to the elephants. "Oh you're happy . . ." he says to one elephant. "Hear that?" he asks as the elephant makes a low noise, "That's a happy sound," he reports. "That's a good sound."

---

[1] **Hackenberger:** [hækənbɜrgər]
[2] **ingrown feet:** an uncomfortable condition of the foot
[3] **husbandry:** animal care

A Trunk-Foot Salute

But can elephants really be happy? Do animals have feelings? If so, are their feelings the same as people's feelings? There's a big discussion about this subject. Many people who work closely with animals say that they do have feelings and can experience happiness. These people think animals are just like humans. Other people are not so certain.

Predict

On the next page you will read about one way that Mike Hackenberger makes elephants feel good. What do you think it is? Scan page 10 to check your answer.

There is one thing that everyone agrees on when they talk about elephants. Elephants seem happier—and safer—if their home in the zoo or circus is very similar to their life among their herd in the wild. Today, zoos work hard to make elephants feel as 'at home' as possible.

Hackenberger also talks to the elephants, and this may help comfort them. "Head over, let's go kids," he says to a group of elephants. "Let's go, **Fatman**![4] Let's go...watch yourself," he says with a smile. He also encourages the animals as they move along, "We're walking, guys. Come on, **Funnyface**,[5] good boy," he says.

---

[4]**Fatman:** a pet name that Hackenberger uses for a particular elephant

[5]**Funnyface:** a pet name that Hackenberger uses for a particular elephant

According to Hackenberger, the training of elephants has improved in recent years. He explains, "I'll tell you . . . ten, fifteen, twenty-five years ago, some of the **techniques**[6] were a bit **barbaric**.[7] We've **walked away from**[8] that...society's walked away from [treating animals like that]." That's news that makes everybody happy.

---

[6]**technique:** a way of doing something that needs skill
[7]**barbaric:** very unkind
[8]**walk away from:** leave behind; forget

One important fact about elephants is that they are social animals. This means that they usually live in families and herds. They need other elephants. Therefore, if they are alone for a long time, they seem to be unhappy and they can start to act in an unusual way.

Hackenberger talks about one elephant, called **Limba**.[9] Limba was alone for 30 years in a zoo in northern **Quebec**,[10] and she didn't do very well by herself. Hackenberger then tells the story of how two other elephants came to live with Limba. They were only two days old at the time. He thinks Limba 'fell in love' with the two young elephants. He also feels that is the reason Limba became happier, and more like a normal elephant.

---

[9] **Limba:** [lɪmbə]
[10] **Quebec:** a part of Canada

Limba fell in love with the two young elephants.

When he is training elephants, Hackenberger talks to them a lot. He's very gentle with them as well. Most importantly, he lets them do things that they do when they are free, in the wild.

For example, elephants love to swim and play in the mud. "Do you, you want to go swimming?" Hackenberger asks the elephants. "**Absolutely**,"[11] he answers for one of them as the elephant actually **nods his head**![12] "Let's get in the water," he says and takes them to the mud hole. The animals really seem to like this pleasant activity.

---

[11]**absolutely:** yes(!); of course!
[12]**nod (ones) head:** move one's head up and down to say yes

So what is the answer to the question: How can people keep elephants happy when they are in captivity? For Hackenberger, the answer is not difficult. He believes that elephants need to learn how to be elephants, just as they are in the wild.

"Are they trained? " he asks a person visiting the zoo. "I think so," she replies." "They're trained to be elephants!" he explains. He then tells one of his very large friends, "Just be an elephant!" With Hackenberger's help, it certainly seems as though his animals are very, very happy elephants!

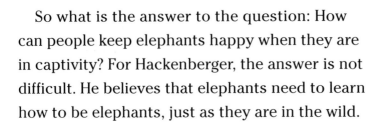

Summarize

What does Hackenberger think about how to keep elephants happy? Summarize this in one sentence.

After You Read

1. On page 4, the word 'gentle' means:
   A. lively
   B. angry
   C. wild
   D. kind

2. There is one question about elephants that people _____ agree on: can elephants be happy?
   A. will
   B. cannot
   C. do
   D. can

3. Which is NOT one way Hackenberger tries to makes his elephants healthy and happy?
   A. He talks to them.
   B. He checks their teeth and feet.
   C. He takes them to the circus.
   D. He trains them well.

4. A good heading for page 6 is:
   A. Man Trains Elephants to Make Happy Sounds
   B. Trainer and Elephants Happy at Seattle Zoo
   C. Trainer Talks to Elephants Too Much
   D. Elephants Are Happy with Caring Trainer

5. Most people who work with animals think that animals:
   A. have feelings
   B. are always happy
   C. are happier than children
   D. cannot have feelings

6. On page 8, who is 'they'?
   A. trainers
   B. feelings
   C. animals
   D. people

7. Society has walked away from _____ animal training techniques.
    A. easy
    B. unkind
    C. good
    D. any

8. What is the meaning of 'unusual' on page 14?
    A. good
    B. bad
    C. boring
    D. happy

9. Why did Limba fall in love with the young elephants?
    A. Because elephants love all young things.
    B. Because elephants are social animals.
    C. Because young elephants are good trainers.
    D. Because she enjoys living alone.

10. Which of the following is something elephants do in the wild?
    A. swim and play in the mud
    B. communicate with people
    C. play together with trainers
    D. fall in love with people

11. What does Hackenberger believe about making elephants happy in captivity?
    A. Elephants can't be happy in a zoo.
    B. Elephants are happy anywhere they can be elephants.
    C. Elephants are happy in captivity if they have a trainer.
    D. Elephants are happiest when they are alone.

Be an Elephant Keeper

Every year thousands of young people leave school for a few weeks or months and enjoy an unusual type of educational program. What they learn during this time does not come from books. They learn new things by living in a different country and doing unusual jobs. There are several organizations that help students find the experience they are looking for. The job description chart below shows a few possibilities for students.

Country	Job	Time	Description
India	Teaching young children	Two months	• Teach music and art • Help children to learn how to communicate
Ghana	Health care worker	Three months	• See how doctors work in a less developed country • Help care for some people
Thailand	Saving elephants	Three weeks	• Cleaning elephants • Helping train elephants

A job can be a learning experience.

Students help clean the elephants.

One interesting possibility is helping elephants in Thailand. Most people think of elephants as animals in zoos or circuses. However, many elephants in Thailand are no longer kept in captivity. Now, hundreds of them are homeless. These gentle animals are often found on the streets as they do not have owners to care for them. Although they may look well, they are often in poor health and don't have enough to eat.

One center in Thailand cares for these elephants. It provides a safe and natural living space for them. When they are at the center, they stay in a building but they are still free to walk around. Students come from all over the world to help here. The student helpers work with the elephant keepers. These keepers train the students in caring for the elephants. In the morning, they go to the forest together and lead the elephants to the center. They clean them and give them food. In the afternoon, they take the animals back into the forest for the night. Helping at the center is interesting and the young people learn a lot.

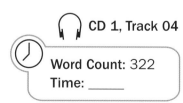

CD 1, Track 04

Word Count: 322
Time: _____

Vocabulary List

absolutely (17)
barbaric (13)
captivity (3, 4, 18)
circus (3, 4, 10)
gentle (3, 17)
herd (2, 10, 14)
humans (2, 4, 8)
husbandry (6)
in the wild (2, 3, 4, 10, 12, 17, 18)
ingrown feet (6)
mud (2, 17)
technique (13)
train (3, 6, 13, 17, 18)
trunk (2, 6)
walk away from (13)
zoo (3, 4, 6, 10, 14)